After an elementary education, Francis Arthur Rawlinson joined the military. He had commissioned ranks and held professional, trade and menial occupations. Francis started his literary endeavours at the beginning of 1996 and had two booklets published. His first tentative attempts needed errata slips coupled with a number of flaws which were eradicated over time with reprints. Francis has since written more than 100 poems in anthologies, three of which were named Editor's Choice by the International Library of Poets. He has also had some short stories published and recently produced a book, *Poems to Ponder, Including Poet in Penury*.

Francis Arthur Rawlinson

# FRANCIS'S INFORMATIVE LYRICS AND POEMS

AUSTIN MACAULEY PUBLISHERS™

LONDON • CAMBRIDGE • NEW YORK • SHARJAH

A CIP catalogue record for this title is available from the British Library.

ISBN 9781398480872 (Paperback)
ISBN 9781398480889 (ePub e-book)

www.austinmacauley.com

First Published 2024
Austin Macauley Publishers Ltd®
1 Canada Square
Canary Wharf
London
E14 5AA

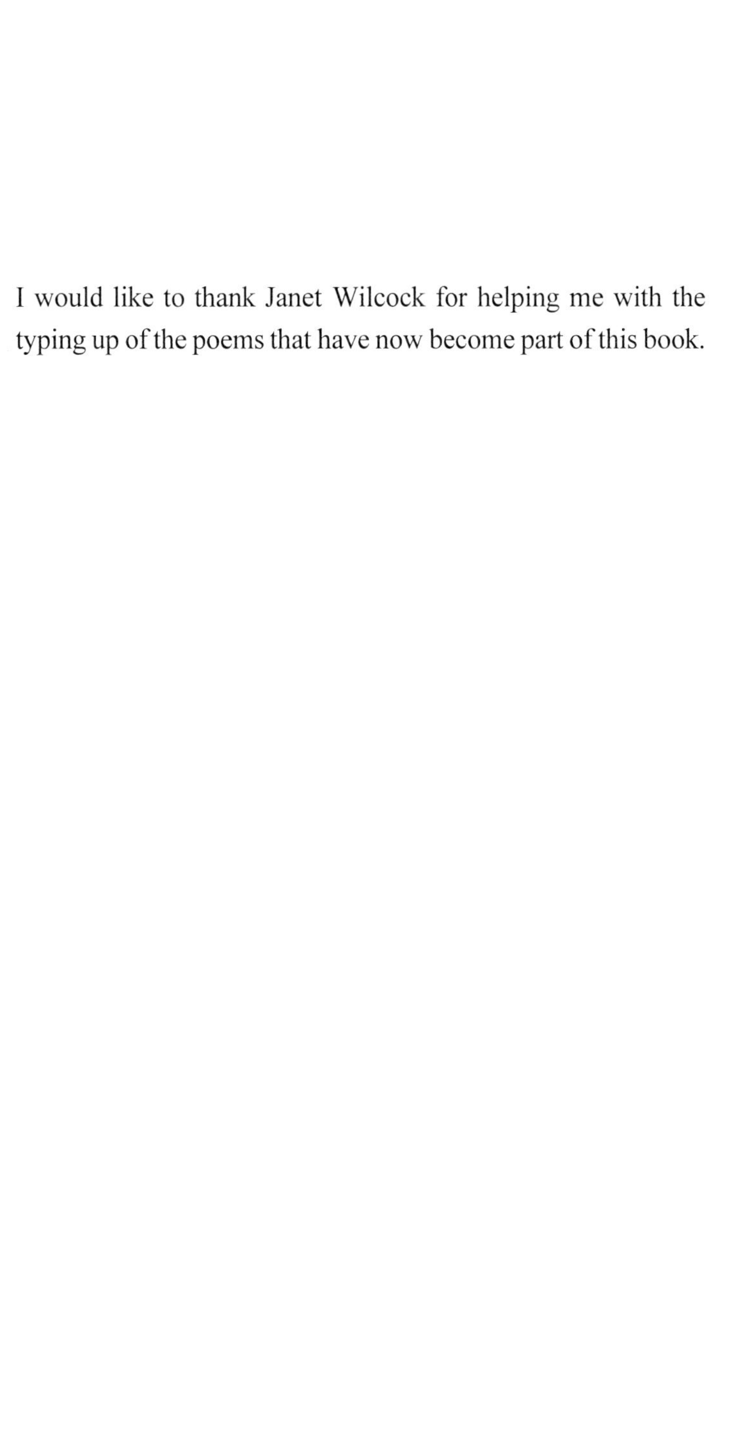

I would like to thank Janet Wilcock for helping me with the typing up of the poems that have now become part of this book.

# Table of Contents


President    13

Date of Birth    14

Self-Taught Wood Worker    15

Control the Atmosphere    16

Sheep Farmer    17

Aging    18

Weasel    19

Women's Lib    20

Bonapart's Short Biography    21

Canary    22

Misogynist    23

Peace    24

Whaling Ship    25

Immigrant Asians    26

For a Good Year    27

Troubled World    28

| | |
|---|---:|
| Horsefly | 29 |
| Call of Nature | 30 |
| Conscience Is Clear | 31 |
| Velocipede | 32 |
| Railway History | 33 |
| Author | 34 |
| Given Enough Rope | 35 |
| Pop Scene | 36 |
| Courtship | 38 |
| Matrimony | 39 |
| A Son of a Share Cropper | 40 |
| Drug Trap | 42 |
| Toilet Training | 43 |
| Cockerel & Baby | 44 |
| Naughty Toddler | 45 |
| Infant | 46 |
| Potty Training | 47 |
| Little Brown Hen | 48 |
| Little Brown Mouse | 49 |
| Jesus Spread the Word | 50 |
| Hoot Nanny Ho Down | 51 |
| Howdy Pard | 52 |
| Bootleg Busker Man | 53 |

Ho Down Party Time — 55

BMW Motors — 57

Speakeasy Hullabaloo — 58

Help the Fallen — 59

Gold Prospector — 60

A Pet Ferret — 61

Country Girl — 62

Shake, Shake Your Body — 63

Homestead Lovers — 64

Old Man River — 65

Arrival of Spring (Sonnet) — 66

Memories of Me and My Dog — 67

Drunken Man — 68

Glutton — 69

The Elderly Crook — 70

Smelly Old Pig — 71

Conceit — 72

Milk Cow — 73

Public Toilet — 74

Tired Old Man — 75

Railway Station — 76

Spider — 77

Cage Birds — 78

Mealtimes 79

Pony and Trap 80

Late Bus 81

Ford Motor Corporation 82

Rail Road 83

A Merry Howdy De Doo 84

Festive Cheer 86

Saturday Soccer 87

Christmas USA 89

Courtship 90

Locomotive Ride 91

Trains and Planes 92

Mass Longevity 93

Military Service 94

Coming of Age 95

Traffic 96

Amorous Loving Encounter 97

Flutters Like a Moth 98

Summer of Sport 99

Point Me in the Right Direction 100

Don't Hold Back 102

Entwined in Your Masculine Arms 104

Wayward Spouse 105

You're the Only One for Me 106

Wild Wales 108

Bloody Sunday Rebellion 109

My Old Cock Sparra 111

Love and Trust 112

The Vicar's Daughter 113

Cattle Drive Country 114

Owl 115

Heartaches and Tribulations 116

Order 117

The Price of Freedom 118

To Lose You 119

Dying Ember 121

Don't Hold Back 122

Homeward Bound 124

Sedentary Vocation 125

The Spider 126

The Future Is Left to Fate 127

Lasting Romance 128

Point Me in the Right Direction 129

Birth of a Baby Boy 130

The Magi Came with Gifts of Praise 131

Please Love Me 133

**No Matter What You Say, You're Mine**     134

**My Lonely Mississippi Belle**     136

**Disciplined**     137

**Drug Scene**     138

**Burning Ambition**     140

**Chaste**     141

# President

In the days Trump had black hair
And of war and politics he was unawares
He was caught on a boxing channel
Most likely with one of his aides
He I surmise used jet black pomade
Because his locks were of a lighter shade
His flaxen blond hair was that of a president
His time is now more fruitfully spent
Commentating on US boxing events.
Leaving Joe Biden, holding the reins of power
It's the Republicans now, come the day come the hour
Law enforcement at breaking point can only glower
Black communities want equal rights
The authorities wont heed their plight
Opportunities for those who are bright.
In university placements or military might
White House, home of the afore mentioned
Where debates and discussion's gain media, press attention
Only the elite can talk war and criminal scam
God bless America and its integrated clan

# Date of Birth

I try to confirm date of birth
But am scorned by zealots with bouts of mirth
I was told I was born, so weak and small
Weighing only a couple of pounds, that's all
Put in bed with a woman trying to conceive
But she died in labour unable to breathe

*I surmise that I shrank from adult stature*

When shaken in the mouth of a shire horse becoming
fractious
Another instance it did happen prior swimming the Atlantic
Breakers shrank when exertion made me tire
I shrivelled into infancy need baby swaddling attire
Just a boy mother unknown
For my misdemeanours, I will have to atone
My conclusion I can only hazard a guess
I leapt from the Hindenburg airship
When known as Count von Zeppelin
If can be confirmed by the press

# Self-Taught Wood Worker

I read an amateur wood worker magazine
When I was inebriated, completely green
Carved, whittled, planed and honed
Took on the mantle of a joiner of old
Then low and behold, a tradesman to behove
Smoothing planes, spoke, shave, the tools of the trade
I will show you how a wooden trestle is made
Wooden artefacts now being constructed
By a hopeful self-taught chippy, from a piece of lumber,
The finished article left a pile of wood shavings
The fruits of his labour didn't make the grade
His endeavours put himself to shame
After all his attempts not to be found
But a heap of sawdust upon the ground!

# Control the Atmosphere

Will the fumes of greenhouse gasses
Affect the populace and diminish the masses
Ice floe's melt and come adrift
Icebergs move and slowly shift
It affects polar bears in the breeding season
Not enough food to feed its cubs
Diversity of climate effects plants and shrubs
No coal fires to make a smog
Asthmatics used to dread the November fog
In summers past, you could foretell it to be fine
Holiday makers didn't have to seek a warmer clime
Thunder storms creating havoc, with unpredictable flash
floods
People lose their chattels, effects and worldly goods
Rivers overflow in raging torrents
People stranded on rooftops which is totally abhorrent
Fire and rescue perform their duties
Police apprehend thieves and "strike it lucky" looters.
All brought about by climate change
All authorities are inundated by the deranged

# Sheep Farmer

Annual round up of sheep from the hills
The sheep farmer has to pay his rent and his bills
Dogs run to and fro to round up the flock
When some are hidden, by moss covered rocks
Ewes bear spring lambs that frolic and play
Sheep to be shorn removing their heavy coats
Fleece combed by bramble, thorn and thistle
Rough coated dog obedient to the whistle
Work like a pack to conduct their mission
Flock moves unaware to a stone enclosure
To be dipped and are given a drench and potion
Faithful old dog now slow with rheumatics
No more earns its keep, its end is dramatic

# Aging

My next-door neighbour has passed away
To offer my condolences, is all I can say
On first name terms and casual passing
A collection, for the floral tribute is in the offing
He was a pleasant man, always laughing
Last time we met he was pale and withdrawn
As Covid-19 became the norm

Others have left the sheltered housing block
As tempus fugit catches up, or not
A care home for the elderly that's your lot!

# Weasel

The dog had a weasel concealed in its mouth
I released it and gave it the run of the house
It liked to clamour up the leg of my pants
When seated incumbent, it licked my ear
It made a home under the kitchen drawers
It took to living indoors, it came to no harm
The Whippet and Mustelidae became firm friends
A dusting of flee powder killed infestation, red mite
The little imp knows I don't tell lies
It ran under the sole of my shoe, hence its demise

# Women's Lib

I feel like a bird confined to a cage
My spouse gets enraged if I want to change
To fly the nest is a latest quest
A show or theatre with my better half
Or a ballroom dance studio, will do for a start
To refresh my latent forgotten repertoire
Freedom for this home alone
Let me free to wonder and roam
Let's party in clubland free and unfettered
Equal rights for women the scene, couldn't be bettered
Took a course in college and gained a degree
My grumpy old partner seems more at ease
I am now more assertive and do as I please

# Bonapart's Short Biography

Who was this small tubby fart?
Known to many as Napoleon Bonapart
His armies plundered, raped and pillaged
He was defeated by the English at Waterloo
Incarcerated on the Isle of Elba, by Egbert's army
Moved to St Helena was to be his fate
To recall past events of this little man
One of the remarks, he reportedly said
"Not tonight Josephine" when he went to bed.
This semi-impotent fought battles of gore and blood
Sat seated on his white stallion, rallying his troops
This military might, in his thigh high boots
His podgy paunch, was the effort of his cooks
He acknowledged them with words of praise
In future hopes, his marshals will rule and reign.

# Canary

The bird lay dead on the cage floor
Its warbling trill heard no more.
Death of such beauty be its fate
A replacement is needed so, post haste
To give solace and comfort
Salvaged with utmost grace
Such infinitive size bringing love and joy
From a twittering cock canary
Time now fills a deep void

# Misogynist

The man was a loner be it of sorts
Was he fulfilled or an outcast shunned and forlorn
A misogynist from the day he was born
Treated women with disdain and scorn
In the changing room, he was furtive
Secretive and shy, ignored by others
Couldn't look you straight in the eye
Suffered some impediment that makes women cry

# Peace

When the hostilities end and abate
The vanquished subdued filled with hate
Prisoners congregate to await their fate
Victors throng in mass
Now a lowly conquered lower class
Stripped of all worldly goods and shackles
Gained from winning all those battles!
Losers pray for, to seek redemption
And hope for liberty from detention
Religious teachings count for naught
What lies ahead leaves them both scared and fraught
As they partake in their meagre meal
Hunger pangs they take what they can steal
Their release date is determined by the hierarchy
To join their relatives back home in 'Blighty'
They celebrate their freedom, with a joyous party

# Whaling Ship

Sail the seas in a westerly breeze
For blubber to feed the populations needs
The lookout shouts from his crow's nest height
For the crew at rest to rally on site
"There she blows" a leviathan in sight!
The whaling master sees red in its eye,
Long boats are lowered to engaged the whale
From the mother ship lashed by a gale
The harpoon thrower, a giant of a man
Engages the beast with his spear like lance
Like modern matelot, from mainland Japan
With modern cannons so advanced
Take on the mammoth, with its oily smell
The slaughter ground is covered in blood and gore
Now shout in exuberance on the sea shore!

# Immigrant Asians

Asian night workers in a cotton mill
Bring their food prepared in a curry tin
They warm their fodder on a heated plate
Scribble letters to relatives who live far away
Ramadan approaches a time of fast
Their vegetarian meals, you can't surpass
They starve themselves, no food allowed
Tending the frames where cotton is wound
Walking around in their flimsy, sandal footwear
Wash their feet, before kneeling in prayer
Some have a prayer mat compass attached
Listen to Allah they are the words of the Iman
Pray facing the directions detailed by the Koran
Flip flops tread softly on the hardwood floor
Work over early morning as they file out the door
Home to partake in a sumptuous repast
Ramadan has ended, Halal meat and rice
Then a trip to the Mosque will have to suffice

# For a Good Year


Let the trumpets sound,
The coming of spring! Loud the bells ring!
Rosh Hashanah, is the New Year and a holiday in the offing
Yom Kippur the day of atonement
Many festivals throughout the year!
Then at the wailing wall so as not to pry
Just listen to the incantations by the Rabbi
Then off to the synagogue to worship and pray
Be it the Sabbath, their holy day
In the Holocaust, Jews died by the million
At the hands of Adolph Hitler, a Nazi villain
Those that survived give thanks for a L'ashana Tovah
For having a good year, pray to Jehovah

# Troubled World

We are told daily in the media press
Of how the world is in a terrible mess
Different religions, different creeds
Have warring factions, and brave deeds
Colour prejudice altogether rife
Can we trust an unsatisfied wife?
Sporting icons constantly in the news
Bigots and charlatans air their views
The Monarchy is failing and on its uppers
Like the ship Sir Galahad it's been scuppered
The Churches fading and of not much concern
Will the powers that be ever lean?
Celebrating dignitary with their puerile banter
The penal system has a lot to answer
Laxity of crimes of murder and high treason
A hangman's rope is what is needed
Islamic countries that practice decapitation
Bring little solace, to the aggrieved relation.

# Horsefly

Beelzebub scouting flesh
With its bedlam eyes
A nasty nip, gives much surprise
This carnivorous imp of summer climes
Sits on many cow pats before it dies
Parody of a poem I can't locate
If can be traced, inform me, don't hesitate.

# Call of Nature

A young lady ran and boarded a train
She was soaked to the skin, trying to avoid the rain
(It was in the days of compartment trains)
No corridors, toilet facilities, or refreshment car
The train lumbered along like a slithering snake
The girl was overcome by the call of nature
A gentleman sitting opposite came to the rescue
Removed his trilby hat and issued instructions
Incontinence she had to crouch and stoop
Then emptying her twat into a trilby hat
The man poured the contents through the open window
No-one was aware of the little debacle
It was the same as transporting cattle!

# Conscience Is Clear


Wearing new Sunday clothes every day of the week
Itinerants bed in shop doorways, their clothes reek
Effete medical staff prescribe a couple of small units a week
Burley building workers imbibe enough to make them sleep
Complainers and moaners with their idol demeanours
Look down on menial tasks carried out by cleaners
Jealousy and envy by those with their tiring tirades
They don't understand how monies are accrued and made
Adolf Hitler killed thousands of cripples and paraplegics,
Deranged Jews and the infirm,
Who couldn't help the way they are made,
Millions of idlers put up a talking charade
Trying to impart knowledge that will only bring shame.
Psychiatrist's study the depths of the mind
Medication and treatment, is what is prescribed
Patients don't comprehend they are being taken for a ride
Hearing voices, hallucination's people deride
Kindly old people try to placate and chide
It's just a troubled conscience
Why not give religion a try?

# Velocipede

Fitted a petrol tank to a frame
Handlebars brakes and two wheels
An engine that's made purely of steel
A kick start motor clinches the deal
A prototype motorbike like as such
The first name if you want to take heed
Be it a motorised skeleton velocipede
You need a brain like that of the Greek Aristotle
Let in the clutch and give it more throttle
On unadopted roads, you get a bumpy ride
This new invention of the road fills you with pride
Solid rubber tyres complete this mechanical beast
At this time and place, petrol pumps are few and far between
You have to take stock to obtain gasoline
Who to praise or give accolades
For such an ingenious product that's man made
Apply the brakes and sound the horn
Rue the day, jay walkers were born
Internal combustion engine, let's think of a motto
It was invented by a great thinker like Nicholas Otto

# Railway History

Surveyors worked as they surveyed the terrain
To lay railway lines to carry a train
Industrial undertakings taking on a different view
Green pastures take on a different hue
People said the first train looked silly
A small insignificant Puffing Billy
The steam engine vehicle churned out oily black smoke
The hard-working fireman had to shovel in coal
Steam escaped from the hissing valves
Onlookers cheered as they enjoyed themselves
As engineering's now greatly improved
Hecklers and Luddites now don't intrude
Diesel and electric of the present generation
Improved amenities are now available on the rail station
Great constructions built where trains are terminated
Tunnels are hewn rail viaducts are completed
Signal boxes and signals keep movement unrestricted
For avoiding fares, culprits will be taken to court,
Sentenced and be convicted for avoiding the system

# Author

Hank Janson a American author, so famed
His novel's brought him fortune and acclaim
In Blighty his writings were put to shame
The magistrate, a stubborn old goat
Saw his books were obscene and count for nought
He ordered them to be destroyed
Leaving ardent fans angry and annoyed
Other writers emulate his style
Using Hanks logo making one smile
A six thousand pound summery fine
And six months in prison to bide his time

# Given Enough Rope

The captured buccaneer faced the hangman's rope
For his crimes at sea, he had no hope
His friends constructed the wooden gallows
With warped floorboards for decking and matting
The camber part, where the parson stood
Forced the warp level with his podgy body weight
Making the timber flat and straight
The end of the floorboards jammed the trapdoor
The cleric installed his weight in his pulpit
Thrice they tried to hang the culprit
Bringing him struggling out of his cell
Was he a chosen felon under gods spell
The trapdoor worked perfectly without a priest
These multiple hangings will have to cease
Giving the Bristol seafarer his release

# Pop Scene

Fans sing famous verses as they sway back and forth.
Arms held aloft swinging to and fro
Pop musicians pluck and strum their electric guitars
Artists gyrating, for the masses to admire.

Groupies join in the musical tirade
Will it make number one on the hit parade?
Harmonious girls singing, the accompanying backing group
Pop stars entertain in his gaudy suit
Will their rehearsal ever bear fruit?

Arose from obscurity, playing in pubs and bars
New they are able to buy expensive cars.
The press and the media report and acknowledge
Smutty lyrics now cause undue concern
Music journals give a favourable review
Taking top accolade in the charts with something new.

Groupies join in this musical tirade
Will it make number one in the hit parade?
Harmonious girls singing, the accompanying backing group
Pop star entertains in his gaudy suit
Will their rehearsal ever bear fruit?
Arose, from obscurity playing in pubs and bars
Now they are able to buy expensive cars.

The press and the media report and acknowledge
Smutty lyrics now cause undue concern
Music journals give a favourable review
Taking top accolade in the charts with something new.
Talking top accolade in the charts with something new.

# Courtship

I love you like a brother
For me, there is no other
I want to kiss and hold you
Until we become ardent lovers
My family urge me to tie the knot
Up 'til now I am happy with my lot
Rushing to do things is not my scene
I think of things that might have been
Hoping to make a token mark
When snuggled up close in the park
With arms entwined in the dark
Love strikes that magic fleeting spark
Bats flit erratically through the night
Just missing the head and causing fright
That is the place that I love most
On the English Riviera, Devon coast

# Matrimony

She came from a poor neighbouring quarter
Now this neat and trim attractive daughter
Men stop to admire her feminine aura
Be it but a dream we'd all like to court her
Building workers whistle as she passes by
She disregards the beholding to the eye
Her clothes are pristine Dior or Quant
Elegance personified, you can tell at a glance
Let's hope our meeting will lead to romance
Holding hands with kindred affection
Tentative remarks of sexual suggestion
Now we are amorous for our forthcoming betrothal
Ancient Brits covered themselves in blue woad
My lovely lady a sight to behold
Blanco white for this matrimonial tryst
Even if you have to fork out money, hand over fist
A church service is what's now required
A parsons blessing then a ride in a carriage
Proud father having paid for a luxury lavish marriage

# A Son of a Share Cropper

This snakebite drinking hard working hillbilly
The son of a share cropper, some thought was silly
But the highfalutin' gentry guess was elementary
They didn't know what went on in his head
As he schemed and planned as he lay in his bed

He thought what to do on his arid plot of land
As he had noticed black gold oozing up through the sand
His crops were sickly and of no further use
He had to sustain himself,
On his long horned steers cow juice
A petroleum company files for the rights
To put up oil derricks, they toiled day and night
He got a percentage of the mineral rights
This rich share cropper on his new found wealth
This man of achievement who had bettered himself

Auto-mobiles and yachts were of no use to him
He liked to laze by the pool and go for a swim
Scanty clad women were out on the mooch
He was taken for a ride

When he had imbibed too much hooch
He became worn and weary, having played the field
Opulence and grandeur no longer appealed

An old log cabin in a forest or a glade
Pick a few cob-nuts, weed and hoe,
Lean on a spade to have blow
Chop up some kindling, if you have no axe to grind
Making fuel for the fire to give piece of mind

# Drug Trap

The police are trying to call the shots
To put an end to Heroin and Cannabis snout
But touts still thrive and ply their wares
Leaving the constabulary embittered and unawares
School yard touts and on street corners they sell their wares
And the police make a lightening raid
Girls sell their bodies to satisfy their needs
Madams and minders, don't take much heed
Mind and body crave for illegal substances
Confusion in the brain, of the helpless psychotic
Visit a clinic for medical treatment
Methadone substitute is a drug replacement
Junkies fall and lie by the wayside
In squalor and filthy communes
While upper crust gentry play a different tune
Pop stars are noted for taking drugs per se
An example to kids and youth of today
How to deter such weakness of will
And get your kicks, without injection or amphetamine pill

# Toilet Training

Sitting perched upon the toilet seat
Until your 'business' is complete
Nothing more or else to do
You'll feel much better when you have had a poo

# Cockerel & Baby

The Cockerel started the day with pride
Cock-a-doodle it cried
The sleeping baby opened up its eyes
It wanted its mother and cried and cried

# Naughty Toddler

The toddler pushed its doll in its pram…
The toddler let it go, and away it ran.
His big sister managed to get a hold
And chastised her, and did scold.

# Infant

The infant liked to suck on its dummy
When lay in its pram, with its fluffy bunny
Until picked up and cuddled by its adoring mummy.

# Potty Training

Eeny Meeny Miney Mo
Put the baby on the poe
When it's done, wipe it's bum
Eeny Meeny Miney Mo

# Little Brown Hen

Higgledy-Piggledy little brown hen
Hasn't laid an egg since, I don't know when
"This won't do" the farmer's wife said
She took out an axe and chopped off its head
Said the farmer "A headless chicken's no use to me,
Unless you pluck out its feathers and cook it for tea!"

# Little Brown Mouse

Higgledy-Piggledy little brown mouse
Lived in a hole she has for a house,
Under the skirting, she would steal
Then into the larder, for a tasty meal

# Jesus Spread the Word

Jesus our God and Saviour
Trod this earth to spread God's Word
He spoke to the masses and the multitude
Performing many miracles showing He is Christ
He spoke of the evil wickedness of man
Denouncing charlatans and false witnesses as a sham
Hatred and bigotry we try to overcome.
To impart the Lord's blessing to every man
Let us all rejoice in the Word of God
Whilst we are still about on this mortal ground
Let us all seek sanctuary in the Lord's teachings
And rejoice in acknowledging His preaching
Make us all content with what life has to offer.
Not letting the Devil's work of greed and avarice proffer
Do not decry or belittle your fellow men
Seek counsel in the scriptures if you have the yen
The power of prayer can ease a troubled mind
In the praise of God will benefit all mankind
In thoughts and misgiving, we must all try to defy
Lewdness and depravity we must smite in the eye
Blasphemy and jealousy we must fight to the end

Trust in the saviours teachings to make righteous amends
Let us all seek sanctuary in the grace of God
With His holy blessings and everlasting love

# Hoot Nanny Ho Down

Mississippi honky-tonk rhythmic blues
Put on those high heel dancing shoes.
Don't sit there musing get off your fat butt
Get in the mood and dance and strut,
Clap your hands and tap your heels,
Give a hoot or a holler whatever appeals

*Hoot nanny ho down*
*Hoot nanny ho down*
*Hoot nanny ho down*
*Hoot nanny ho down*

Listen to the rhythm of a hoochy coo guitar
Kick drums, harmonica, a buzzing kazoo
The melodious rendition will entertain you
Kick up your heels to gladden and amuse
Just a country boy with no lovin' Mammy
Let loose amongst cow girls at a ho down hoot nanny

Love is in the air romance is nigh
A peck on a cheek will have to suffice
Holding hands together at a hoot nanny ho down
Buckskin clad cowgirls their interest aroused
By a cowpokes' macho display
Who stood out from the crowd

# Howdy Pard

I want to sing an old country song
Where all the howdy pards can sing along
Clap your thighs and tap your heels
A rousin' medley do what you feel
A country ho down that steals the show
Such wild merriment! It's all systems go.

Banjo strums a harmonious rendition
Dance like a Siox war dance, performing an audition.
Gather up courage with a few fingers of rye
To approach my intended the apple of my eye
Let your hair down my sweet chickadee
And let the world know you belong to me
Courting and a kissing as you melt in my arms
I am a weakling, enticed by your charms

Let's dance 'till morn at this old lindy hop
Let's hope you agree when I plight my troth.
Let's dance 'till morn at this old lindy hop
Let's hope you agree when I plight my troth.

# Bootleg Busker Man

Going to get away on that choo, choo train
The folks where I am seem to be all insane.
Find a place in which to live and dwell
Forgetting the past it was a living hell.
Find a woman for which to live and share
My plans are now known, laid stark and bare

Ride that train to pastures and fields anew
As I strum the old five string guitar for you
onlookers appear from near and a far.
As I slack my thirst from an old whisky jar
Prohibition put an end to this hullabaloo
But I still partake in the odd one or two

*Harmonica and kick drums on my one man show*
*I make a good living I want all to know*
*Bystanders and onlookers surround and applaud for such*
*gratuities I thank the good lord*

Sitting on the front porch with my old pipe smoking
Granny remembering the days we kicked up a hoot nanny
A song bird sings it's rendition to the setting sun
Nightfall descends on this son of a gun
Playing a harmonica with such raucous aplomb

Dusk descends now it's time to hit the sack
We all go inside of this old tumbled down shack,
Kissing and a cuddling my pretty hoochy-coo,
Smiles as she surrenders meekly to my masculine wiles
My lovin' baby, my sweet honey child

54

# Ho Down Party Time

My old log cabin in a forest glade
Digging and planting crops, with a digging aid
Work up an appetite doing hard graft
Ploughing and a tilling, with a stubborn old mule
Kicking over the traces acting the fool

Chewing and a puffin on my old corn cob pipe
Hearty repast on 'chicklings' and greens
Chopping up logs for kindling wood
Dance at the ho down cutting a rug
Fiddlers, fiddle instruments under the chin
Bowing the catgut strings on their violin,
Kick up a raucous making a merry din

Fatten up the hog, for a feast in the offing
Thanksgiving a time of merriment, jest and banter
Girls dance and twirl at a merry canter
A sip of whisky all augers to the good
Teenage girls bring in new fresh blood
Whilst old timers applaud with clap of hands
Tipsy drunk revellers stand tall, like Custer's last stand

Old grannies sit and listen to the sound of the band
Sit giggling and cackling with joyful glee,
Sitting astride some bony, old timers, knee

Go to powder their nose sneeze into a frilly hankie
Take a drop or two of old mothers ruin
Ponder what lies a foot, what lies a brewing,
Courting couples sit billing and a cooing

Things come to an end folks leave willy nilly
Turn up your coat collar, as the evening gets chilly

# BMW Motors

I like to travel on holiday by car
To places of interest both near or far
Places of interest which to admire the view
Perused through the window of my spanking new B.M.W

A luxury car of skill and scrupulous selection
By men who work to precise engineering perfection,
Pistons and sprockets, fan belt or overdrive
Many years of dedication of men no longer alive

A beast of ingenuity that pleases the eye
The sheer beauty and symmetry could make you cry
A long waiting list for the rich and wealthy few
Then a proud owner of a new model B.M.W

Engine purrs like a kitten when given a saucer of milk.
Drives like a dream runs as smooth as silk.
Automatic or manual, whichever is preferred
To criticise or find fault is absolutely absurd
Auto-mobile pundits on TV's Top Gear Full of praise for
BMW,
Saying they are reasonably priced and not too dear

# Speakeasy Hullabaloo

Hi de hi, ho dei ho, enjoying a riotous alcohol fuelled show
In this notorious drinking, Irish owned drinking shebeen
Ignoring prohibition on the speak-easy scene
Bottle after bottle of illegal hootch
Served by wealthy dressed publican crooks
In this notorious iniquitous drinking den

Scantily clad girls enticing the drunken men
Revered by many who canoodle showing their spunk
Cigar and tobacco smoke fills the air, congesting the lungs
Tipsy on grog in this man made smog
Headache eased by the hair of the dog
Dress code is strict evening suit and dicky bow tie
Saluting each other with a "mud in your eye"
The cops encroach on this hullabaloo scene
Cop cars arrive their sirens scream
Heads bludgeoned with batons make a gory scene
Barrels of beer axed to flow down the drain
Tax evading crooks jailed in the pen, or homes for insane
While negligent authorities are left to appropriate blame

# Help the Fallen

Sing Hallelujahs don't let Satan's work fool you
Look up to God in heavens high
Conformation in bread and chalice wine
God's holy road is the road to take
Disregard charlatans and users on the make
Tread the path of righteousness
Following God's holy creed
Admonish avarice jealousy and greed
Sing Hallelujahs in joy of God's spoken word
Rejoice in God, the Lord's good works
Pray for the less fortunate
And those fallen by the way
Do not appropriate ridicule or shame
Hold out an outstretched arm
Vagaries of life are to blame
Sing hallelujahs, in praise of Gods good name

# Gold Prospector

Down in the Klondyke known for its gold
Prospectors toil until they grow old
Panning in the rivers or streams for grains of ore
Working from dawn until the onset of dusk
California gold rush to stake your claim
Get lucky and hit pay dirt and strike it rich

Brothels and saloon bars with your new found wealth
Now ride in auto-mobiles having bettered oneself
Pick and a shovel work your but off
Diggin for nuggets ridiculed by those who can only scoff

Visit the barbers for a trim and a shave
Clean up your act, lonely are the brave
The solitary life of these woe begotten men
Seek the company of woman in bordellos, If they have the
yen
Play poker for high stakes, at the table in bars
Losing or winning fortunes at the turn of a card
Rheumatism puts an end to this monastic way of life
Left to rot in solitude, with no loving wife.

# A Pet Ferret

Ever since I was a slip of a boy
I was attracted and amused by the animal mustelids
Commonly known as the fitches or ferret
Often given a bad name it doesn't merit
Scrupulously clean in its environment
Uses one corner for which to spend a penny
Debris removed daily and replaced with a scoop of litter or
sand
Some are deterred by the bodily scent or odour
Others enthralled by the farmyard aroma
Babies may give a playful nip or bite
A veterinarian to remove the fangs, if causing fright
Feed soaked biscuit meal (kibble) for it to nibble
A raw egg may be preferred for a treat, or a morsel of raw
red meat;
A water container fastened to the cage front,
To keep it hydrated, stop it choking on dust
A roomy cage for indoor use, obtained from a pet store
Outdoors a large wooden cub or hatch may fit the bill
Wood, wool or paper shredded bedding fits the purpose
If handled frequently becomes tame and playful
A pet that's loyal and loving for many years to come
A brownish polecat with black eyes, or white with a pink
eyed albino seems just right
Books on the subject are easily obtained
Be you a fanatic or beginner, whatever your age

# Country Girl

Over and over and over again
I'm a country girl, a lover of men
As I strum my 5-string guitar
Men admire me, from near and afar
They take me for jaunts in their auto-mobiles
As we stroll hand in hand
Through pastures and fields
I'm a country girl lover, who sings from the heart
With my handsome guy, nothing can tear us apart
On a Saturday night at the local hop,
The dawn plays a medley of country pop
As I kick up my heels in my ho-down attire
My handsome beau sets my heart ablaze on fire
My ardent lover in his Stetson hat
With the feline grace, of a mountain cat,
He sets my heart racing with a pitter-pat
I am a victim enamoured by his charms
I feel content in his strong masculine arms
We ask the preacher man to swear an oath
To join us together, to unite us both
Now on the rocky road of matrimony of life
A faithful cowpoke and his loving wife.

# Shake, Shake Your Body

Over and over and over once again
What will transpire from the ink of a pen
Rock and roll rhythms will no doubt ensue
Let us all dance to a raptures review
Shake, shake your body and give us a treat
Keep the dance going and move your feet
Wave your arms in wild disarray
As a band of musicians with abandon play
Gasp for a breath as fatigue sets in
Sit down for a rest from the melodious din
Select a partner with whom to share
To make a matching compatible pair
With rock and roll medleys
Going far into the night
The thronging mass is a wondrous sight
Torsos gyrate to such a hullabaloo
Bodies then disappear leaving just a few

# Homestead Lovers

High Ho, fiddle de de, I don't let girls get sassy with me
Holding hands as we go for a walk
Testing her demeanour, with baby talk
Stop to carve our names on a tree
A loving heart, etched out by me
Sitting together on a green grassy knoll
Making daisy chains to please my amours moll
Two loving fugitives who are deeply in love
Stealing her affections to kiss and caress
Fumbling in the buttons, causes some little distress
A passing stranger, a smile a mile wide
On seeing the loving couple kissing like Bonnie and Clyde
Making their way back to the old home stead, back home
For a chicken chowder, and hog on the bone
Strong black coffee simmering in a coffee percolator
Hoping to make it with my honey baby, sooner or later

# Old Man River

The mountain streamed by melting snow
Winds and wends, its torrential flow
Now as it becomes murky that was once clear
As it tumbles over a man-made weir
Conservation has made things better
Out even they can't make water wetter
The peace and tranquillity of fathoms deep
Where weeping willows, gracefully weep
Where poets and bards have all enthused
And some may have become mentally bruised
With reeds and rushes enough to conceal a trout
Whilst patient anglers wait and sit it out
Be it a rippling eddy or raging flood
Sometimes bad, be it sometimes good
Debris and flotsam survive the deluge
Swept out to sea by waves from Neptune
That small trickle from a hill side spring
Fed by brooks to mass a stream
All converge on the way to the sea
Where old man river, fades into the estuary

# Arrival of Spring (Sonnet)

As another year comes to an end
Another appears in the immediate offing
The winter solstice draws to a close
Spring arrives with its warmer clime
Behold the sights with autumnal views
Leaves on trees, with their different hues
Birds build their nests to procreate and breed
Foraging for food, pecking up seed
The chirping brood soon to fly the nest
Giving their parents' time to preen and rest
Spring flora and its annual wondrous plants
Small mammals at work, like colonies of ants
Food is plentiful and in great supply
God's nature beholding to the naked eye.

# Memories of Me and My Dog

I'm an old be whiskered Honkey-Tonk
Whether be sober or tipsy drunk
On my lonesome, I spend my time
Wishing for my long gone dead wife
It's a long weary road to travel
Now long in the tooth, can't fit shingles on my hovel
Date of birth, no written paper proof
Born when the corn harvest didn't bear fruit
People starved for lack of food during this interlude
My old dog scratching it's infected behind
Moves itself and makes for the shade
It's weary bones stiff, since it last caught a rabbit
My loyal old partner makes me laugh or cry
On our excursions to the general store
Flour and oil to make a meat jerky meal,
My faithful cur takes what it can steal
Remembering memories of times harking way back
Take a snort of Snake Bite, before hitting the sack.

# Drunken Man

The man's wife lived in fear
Her husband was violent after drinking beer
The policeman called and made clear
Mend his ways or its jail for a year

# Glutton

69

The man's wife who was of a plump disposition
Liked nothing more than to enjoy cooking sessions
She boiled and roasted large lumps of mutton
For her fat husband who was a habitual glutton

# The Elderly Crook

The elderly crook was now old and frail
It was his only his age that kept him out of jail
Before the magistrate, he stood to be judged
The blot on his copy book was more than a smudge

# Smelly Old Pig

Smelly old pig with a ring in its nose
Ran to its food trough when the situation arose
It grunted and snorted and did not leave a morsel
It then had a think, then a long thirsty drink

# Conceit

Mirror mirror on the wall
I'm so little and I want to be tall
As years passed by I began to notice
My clothes were to small
It cured my neurosis

# Milk Cow

The farmer in Switzerland tethered his cow
To a wooden plank, between its front and back legs
Making it walk in a circle, like it was treading on eggs
To forage and graze as it went round
This rotund pasture daily re-situated
Making the milkmaid happy and elated

# Public Toilet

In the days of sterling shillings and pence,
It cost a penny for toilet entrance
Now decimal is the current rate
It costs twenty pence to defecate

# Tired Old Man

Tired old man sits in his armchair
The passing of time he is unaware.
No more is he able to gad about
His legs are seized with rheumatic and painful gout

# Railway Station

Train pulls up at the railway station.
Awaiting the arrival of a distant relation
Asking a porter is the train on time?
It is he replied, your waiting on the wrong line

# Spider

The spider weaves its sticky web
Awaiting to snare a fly, it's said!
When caught, it lies there still and dead
Now the spider can be fed

# Cage Birds

The yellow birds perched inside their abode,
Scatter seed upon the living room floor.
The singing miscreants in their wire cage,
Make the cleaner fly into a rage!

# Mealtimes

Breakfast time, fry-up and bowl of porridge oats,
Mid-day, biscuits and a cuppa
Lunchtime, toasted teacake and a coffee
Dinner, cooked meal with a glass of wine
Supper, hot chocolate for bedtime sipping

# Pony and Trap

The small pony pulling a cart
Lifted its tail and made a fart
Not many people have a pony and trap
Manure for the rose garden, it's had a crap

# Late Bus

A long queue waiting for the bus
It was very late it was causing a fuss
Drivers off sick, caused by some virus
Overworked staff, plagued by tiredness

# Ford Motor Corporation

I viewed the showroom to see what I could afford
I viewed the display and decided on a Ford
Cars through the ages from a model 'T' Ford
Peruse vintage prefects or Anglia's from the days of yore

Fiesta's and Focus are new on the scene
Handling and mobility runs like a dream
Listen to the sales pitch, "you don't have to be rich
If your credits good, you can obtain without a hitch"

Ford 8 and popular of bygone days
Are no longer seen on the Kings highways
Now obsolete but have served their purpose
Capri's are no longer in demand, like a four ranged circus

Mondeo's and Escort's appraised on your first meeting with
intense aroma of opulence and luxury seating that assails the
nostrils, and sets the heart beating

The latest model of a noted new Cougar
Internet adds you can still obtain a second-hand Cougar
All made by this household car makers name
Manufactured by this giant Ford Motors fame

# Rail Road

Across the pond they sing this song
A gandy dancer has to be strong
A platelayer is what the limeys term
They are not employed by a USA firm
The wheel tapper tests each wheel with a hammer
With expert ease and purposeful manner
No cracks, no weakness or metal fatigue
Total loyalty is a railroad man's creed
New York city engulfed in a smog
The engineer makes out his daily log
Can't see your hand, in front of your face
Slow the train down to a walking pace

On a murky British November day
Hordes of commuters wend their way
A scarf or face mask excludes the grime
To catch their connections in plenty of time

A platelayer walks on traversing the line
Detonators explode one at a time
Nervous passengers listen with trepidation
All augers well as reach their destination

# A Merry Howdy De Doo

Hot dog, jiggy dog, I feel so tired and weak
Akin to Mark Twain's hopping buckshot laden frog's pitiful
defeat
Watching the gyrating dancers gives my heart a treat
To sit awhile to take the weight of my aching legs and feet
When fully recovered, then I am able to compete
To the rhythm and compulsive, rhythmic, rousing beat

Let's hit the town with a knee slapping ho-down revue
Jitterbugging and kicking up a merry hullabaloo
Brighten up the evening with a snifter or snort a' two
From a jug of moonshine, the devil's evil brew
Jitterbugging and kicking up a hell of a raucous much a do
To reminisce on past conquests and events to mull over and
chew

Hot dog, jiggy dog I feel so tired and worn out and weak
Just to sit awhile to take the weight off my aching legs and
feet
And to reminisce on any conquests or events so to speak
Like Mark Twain's lethargic tainted jumping frog's defeat
Just to sit awhile to take the weight off my aching legs and
feet

Then I'm able to dance and partake
To the rousing, compulsive, rhythmic beat
Then I'm able to dance and partake
To the rousing compulsive rhythmic beat

# Festive Cheer

Christmas comes but once a year
Bringing joy and happiness with festive cheer
Santa's goods to look forward to
Let us all rejoice be it Christian or Jew
A time to reflect on the birth of a boy
To speak lovingly with words of joy
Making the world a better place
Putting all the world to right denouncing hate
Mistletoe and holly for all to see
With baubles and glitter, on the Xmas tree,
Crackers paper hats at Yuletide lunch
A fruit bowl filled with spiced rum punch
Turkey and trimmings on which to dine
Washed down with a bottle of claret wine
Plum pudding with a rich rum sauce
Toasting friends and family with every course
Turkey and trimmings on which to dine
Washed down with a bottle of claret wine
Plum pudding with a rich rum sauce
Toasting Friends and family with every course
Toasting friends and family with every course

# Saturday Soccer

The coach said that I was too undernourished
Small and effete but the opposing team couldn't get the ball
off my feet.
Running down the wing gives the spectators a thrill.
Weaving and twisting on goal attacks, bamboozling full
backs
Putting the ball in the back of the net, leaving the goalkeeper
dismayed and perplexed!
Play up, play up, and play the game putting the opposition to
shame
Away supporters reply with a rousing enthusing chant
If the players were dogs, their tongues would hang out to
pant,
A player lies prone on the ground that's muddy and damp
Needs the bucket and sponge brigade to ease the cramp
Ref intervenes, and orders the unfortunate to be stretchered
off
Booking the sheepish instigator for causing an infringement
Saint John's medic tends, with a bottle of oil of green
liniment
All augers well, until a stale mate seems to ensue
A one-one draw seems deemed to be the order of the day
As the ref blows the whistle for the end of the play
The spectators wind their way through the back street home

With ribald remarks and desultory chants, they will have to
wait for the return match, for a decisive result.

# Christmas USA

Christmas is a time when words have to rhyme
St Nicholas shakes his tin for nickels and dimes
Maceys' store floor walkers tread with stealth
To deprive all their customers of surplus wealth
Christmas products displayed on the shelf
Bringing Christmas cheer when in rude health
For presents for kids in the USA,
Let's see what the red robed phantom has to say
Christmas is a time for the living
Remember the past with thanksgiving
A festive spirit recalled all mankind
Remember the unfortunate and don't be unkind
Next year there will be a similar repeat
A nativity play, washing Jesus feet
While the cops keep traffic flowing,
On 42nd street, icy winds keep blowing
For presents for the kids in the USA,
Let's see what the red robed phantom has to say
Christmas is a time for the living
Remember the past with thanks giving
A festive spirit recalled all mankind
remember the unfortunate and don't be unkind
Next year there will be a similar repeat
A Nativity play, washing Jesus' feet
While the cops keep traffic flowing,
On 42nd street, icy winds keep blowing

# Courtship

The deep throated whisper of the wind
Blow harshly as cold words ring
The icy blast tinges the he cheeks red
Sexual annotations about sharing a bed
Her hair billows by the bracing blow
Her un-rouged cheeks aglow
As the wind lulls itself to hush
It has abated like her embarrassed blush
Entwined in her lovers arms embrace
Heads drawn nearer face to face
Lips touch momentarily for a kiss
A moment her suiter could not miss
Her demeanour now thawed and annulled
By her lovers experience and his bold
Listening to her boyfriend's wiles in a trance
They had both found true romance

# Locomotive Ride

Hear the klaxon sounding
As we steam along the line
Getting there punctually
To hit the dead line
Some get a little shut-eye
As they pass from state to state
Tedium and boredom such a long, long way
Show your tickets the conductor's heard to say
The grandeur of such scenery
As we snake along our way
A photographers paradise
With cine camera with which to play
With designer posture seating
Even though you may not notice,
Legs get a little cramped
Avoid deep legged thrombosis
Make the way down the aisle
Want to use the 'Jon'?
Dispense with your services
Then back where you came from
Passengers mill around the station
Anticipated journey leaves them fraught
Waiting for a locomotive train
A giant juggernaut
Reaching your location time to leave the track
Lugging your luggage won't be going back

# Trains and Planes

Train wheels turning down the track
Covering miles and miles looking back
Snuggle up warm in your winter overcoat
Until you reach your destination the airport
At the air terminal to book your flight,
Some prefer to travel late at night
Even though it's only a short haul hop,
Everybody's got to be frisked by the airport cops
Only take hand luggage you are allowed
Then you won't stand out in the ensuing crowd
Urgent work in progress on the opposite line
Make a bus detour and connection to make up the time
On the return journey from Manchester UK,
The train separates at Preston to Glasgow
The rear coaches to Blackpool North Parade
Down to the beach with a bucket and spade.

# Mass Longevity

London noted for its ceremonies and parades
Of parliamentary discussions and tireless debates
Hordes of photographers, biographers and reporters
Clamouring to get shots of the monarch's sons and daughters
Crowds of rubberneckers to wave and cheer
As the royal entourage gradually gets near
Only a shadow of criminal reported indiscretions
Mafia's and covens of cannibalistic acts and aggressions
The church elders pray with the reverence to God
Go to their graves in ignorance interred under the sod
Military might presume the plight of this country
When scores of insurgents have made surreptitious entry
Elderly women with their childish banter
With undernourished bodies in skimpy apparel
The do-gooders with their infantile thoughts and suggestions
Police executives in their pristine attire
Try to appropriate blame when they come under fire
Military hierarchy with their academic qualifications
Silver spoon fed with their trickery and aspirations

Famed in battles and skirmishes that should never have been
undertaken
In Arabian countries where crime is punishable by
execution,
These lines of enquiry are the only worthwhile solution

# Military Service

I was conscripted at the age of eighteen
To serve my country and the Queen
I sailed to countries far and wide
A fully trained soldier filled with pride
To engage the enemy was the goal
In a Korean conflict fought in Seoul
And in other theatres of war worth a mention
For insubordination spent time in detention

And for serving in Afghanistan
With a limbless amputee,
But for grace of God, it could have been me!
Seconded to the Australian slouch army hat
I did a stint in Vietnam war for UK, Malaysia and Bosnia

Suez and Belize the pioneer corps in Hong Kong
I received the highest honour the Crown bestowed
Inaugurated into many regiments and corps
I imbibed too much ale like brandy sodden bores
Having received my army discharged papers
Reminiscing of days on my valour and my many capers

# Coming of Age

On your 21st year of coming of age,
I will jot down a few notes and to try and fill a page
With rhyme and meter to try and fill a slot,
I will endeavour not to lose the plot,
Editors may come, and editors may go,
But each leave a book to show,
To grace a bookshelf taking pride of place,
To peruse at leisure and try and put a smile on their face,
To recite a poem to children, engrossed and to select one
they love most.
Another time at a later date, that they themselves may want
to narrate.

# Traffic

Traffic congestion on the motorway
A long tailback causes hours of delay
A fatal accident proves to be the cause
Ignoring the crossing and laid down by laws
Another busy time for the over worked traffic police
Having to fathom and surmise what caused such grief
Measurements are taken skid marks and all
Placards are erected for witness to confess
A mention of the case in the daily press
The local rags obituary of whom was laid to rest

# Amorous Loving Encounter

Let's all join in and sing a carousing song
When dancing like lovers in a merry throng,
Let's take a chance and enhance our budding romance
Entwined in each other's warm and tender embrace
To test her demeanour and naive feminine grace
We waltzed and danced till the band stopped playing
Our new found partnership seemed to have made the grade
On our way home, she laid her head on my beating chest
Her female trust in her suitor seemed to have stood the test
Caressing her sylph like body she wilted in my arms
One unbuttoned her dress, I kissed her ripe breast
My knees a tremble my passion aroused, to her submissive
consent
As she succumbed to my ardour our love covered new
ground
Both were gratified as our nuptial we did not try to expound
A matrimonial engagement seemed to be next in the offing
To for two lovers to alley any envy or jealous scoffing

# Flutters Like a Moth

Love is a torment, love is a bind
Love is a burden, love a grind
Love is a spark that concentrates the mind
When bodies unite, love is blind
Love is like a moth attracted to flame
Love gives lovers the urge to do the same
When moths in the wardrobe start to breed,
Lovers in love wish to sow their seed
When the heart flutters like a moth,
And a lover wants to plight his troth
If acceptance is the wishful reply,
Both in harmony together until they die
Loves satisfying and a great joy.
When parents expect a girl or a boy,
Love was so fulfilling, playing its part
Giving lots of affection from a kindred heart
When the heart flutters like a moth,
And a lover wants to plight his troth
If acceptance is wishful reply,
Both in harmony together until they die.
When the heart flutters like a moth,
And a lover wants to plight his troth
If acceptance is the wishful reply,
Both in harmony together until they die

# Summer of Sport

## Cricket

Being picked for the schools cricket team
I was enthralled and, in a dream,
Not being tall enough for my age
Taller boys left out were enraged
The umpire requested middle and leg
My intention was to take the opposition down a peg
As the game proceeded my aggregate was poor
Last man in scoring a pathetic four
Years later when in my pomp and prime
I was chosen to play for my county full time
Amateur but pleased, as pleased as punch
Scoring a century prior close for lunch
Dressed in gloves helmet and knee pads
Like some valiant warrior bedecked in white armour clad
The sound of leather hitting willow
Play up, play up and play the game arousing cheer
Before retiring to the pavilion for a beer

# Point Me in the Right Direction

When you kiss me, you're the most
If it weren't for you, I'd give up the ghost
An invitation in the post
It's my party cause I'm the host

*So point me in the right direction*
*It's only for you I have affection*
*You are my number one selection*
*Baby you are sheer perfection*

If you're lonely and in repose,
You know my number pick up the phone
I will call when you're at home
I don't want you to be alone

*So point me in the right direction*
*It's only for you I have affection*
*You are my number one selection*
*Baby you are sheer perfection*

The nearness of your feminine charm
Makes me want to chance my arm
All you have to do is keep very calm
I won't let you come to any harm

When I'm with you, I feel content
Of happy times and memories spent
Just shout and come hell bent
To be near you I'd pitch a tent

# Don't Hold Back

*I long for you, with all of my might*
*Your kisses seem to be just right*
*Please say I'm on the right track*
*Give your all and don't hold back*

I've tried to draw your attention
Too many times, too often to mention
Won't you please save my plight
And give me comfort through the night

*I long for you with all of my might*
*Your kisses seem to be just right*
*Please say I'm on the right track*
*Give your all and don't hold back*

The warmth of your masculine touch
Is what I long for ever so much
Please don't be so contrite
Entwine our bodies through the night

*I long for you with all of my might*
*Your kisses seem to be just right*
*Please say I'm on the right track*
*Give your all and don't hold back*

A love filled marriage I crave
For you, storm and tempest I'd brave
Mission improbable, it's true
If suspicion gets the best of you

*I long for you with all of my might*
*Your kisses seem to be just right*
*Please say I'm on the right track*
*Give your all and don't hold back*
*Give your all and don't hold back*

# Entwined in Your Masculine Arms

Do you love me I want to know
You make my expectations grow and grow
A simple yes or a simple no will suffice
A kiss on the cheek will break the ice

*Entwined in your masculine arms*
*Let's you savour my feminine charms*
*A lovers tryst in a sweet embrace*
*A contented blush upon my face*
*You captivate me with your manly ways*
*Everything about you I have to praise*

I like to lean my head against your vest
And listen to your heartbeat in your chest
Your charisma and experience captivates
My fondling and kissing makes my legs go
Weak I'm at your mercy lay at your feet

*Entwined in your masculine arms*
*Let's you savour my feminine charms*
*A lovers tryst in a sweet embrace*
*A contented blush upon my face*
*You captivate me with your manly ways*
*Everything about you I have to praise*

# Wayward Spouse

Sing if you want to be heard
Love can express the spoken word
A song can right a wayward wrong
It placates a tension when sung a long
You may have to use the wisdom of Solomon
A little white lie can solve a problem
To get back into your wife's good books
And diffuse those disapproving looks
And love once more is in the air
Making us again a loving pair
To lay in each other's arms to share
Thanking the Lord with a simple prayer
No more will I stray from the fold
But be faithful together until we grow old
To ease the tension of an uneasy house
Hear the confessions of a wayward spouse

# You're the Only One for Me

You're the only one for me
Let's get together and live happily
You're the only one can't you see?
You're the only one for me

*Please won't you heed my plight*
*And help me make it through the night*
*You're the only one can't you see*
*You're the only one for me*

I crave for you madly
And will wait for you gladly
I'm a woman willing and true
I don't mind waiting for you

*Please won't you heed my plight*
*And help me make it through the night*
*You're the only one can't you see*
*You're the only one for me*

I will be faithful and be true
So long as I love and hold onto you
If I search the world over,
I could never find another love as true
*Please won't you heed my plight*

*And help me make it through the night*
*You're the only one, can't you see?*
*You're the only one for me!*
*Please won't you heed my plight*
*And help me make it through the night*
*You're the only one, can't you see?*
*You're the only one for me!*

# Wild Wales

I like to spend my holiday vacation
And take in the sights of rural Wales, by exploration
Anglesey with its attractions and its rural charm
The simple pleasures aroma of a country farm
Where you can barter or tender for country fare
To spend a time daily sunbathing on the beach,
Your tanned body is now complete enjoy a jaunt in rowing
boat or motor launch
Partake in a cream tea, adding inches to the paunch
To view and appreciate the Swallow Falls
As the Welsh people term it Betws-y-Coed
A coach trip to the Snowdonia National Park
And savour the rendition of a soaring lark
Ffestiniog Rail, with a ticket to purchase
Sightseeing such scenic views to enjoy and entertain us
George Borrow the author and writer of Wild Wales,
Entertains and amuses us with his Dydd-da tales
Llandudno a favourite Welsh attraction resort
Where we board our coach to return to our own bed and
home. With a heavy heart and feelings of dejection and
forlorn.

# Bloody Sunday Rebellion

A catholic priest waved a white flag of truce
Gunfire did not abate it was of no use
Bloody Sunday a day of infamy and shame
Aspersions cast on the British armies good name
Stones and missiles thrown at the beleaguered men
Such ferocity and hate with grievous intent
The troops stood their ground, which had to be held
The crowd tended injured, Who lay where they had been
felled
Snatch squads apprehended ring leaders,
Wearing little protection.

Water canon sprayed the melee from a different direction
The ranks of the papist were now decimated and depleted
For the bereaved and the dying killed in the fights,
A holy man prayed and bestowed the last rights.
The military top brass was apportioned the blame
Let's pray for sanity to defeat zealots and the acts of the
insane.
Bloody Sunday a day of infamy and shame

Aspiration on the British army's good name
Snatch squads apprehended ring leader
Wearing little protection.

Water canon sprayed the melee from a different direction
Ranks of the papists were decimated and depleted
For the bereaved and the dying, killed in the fights.
A holy man prayed and bestowed the last rights
The military top brass was apportioned the blame
Let's pray for sanity to defeat zealots and the acts of the
insane.

# My Old Cock Sparra

In the days when strides were tight and narra
Costermongers plied their trade from a barra
Ted's and Mod's were at logger heads
Scooter Mods army in where resplendent in their attire
Pearly Kings and Queens in their Oyster shell buttons to
admire
A Cockney cheeky fella stole fruit from a stall
Making the vendor look impotent and small
The trader hailed a passing Bow Street Peeler
To catch and apprehend, the citrus fruit stealer
Advertising cards in telephone box displays
Ladies of ill repute, show their gaudy wares
Jellied eels on Petticoat Lane; for which they are famed
Old Kent Road another landmark of which to name
Waiting for a cab you need the patience of a saint
Buxom flower sellers they look so attractive and quaint
Pretty girls to be admired
Making an old cock sparras tired heart aglow with fire

# Love and Trust

Hold me tight and never let me go
Cuddle me and my love will flow
As we dance together real slow
Romance is afoot its began to show
I'm a happy girl, I want all to know
I love and trust my strong handsome guy
No one can take his place, even if they try
I remain faithful honest and true
Accepting his finger ring with aplomb
I will cherish it always, for evermore
All that is left is to name the day
The Padre from the pulpit calls the bans
As he names the day with clasped hands
Two people to live together as one
The rocky path of life has began
To share with everlasting love
A contented woman and her loyal man

# The Vicar's Daughter

Throw me in at the deep end
But I don't want to drown
I want to paddle my own canoe
And make it with a babe like you
I'm in very deep water
Trying to make it with a Vicar's daughter
She's conversant with all the Psalms
But she's a temptress in my arms
Her daddy taught her to be honest and true
But she lets me drink champers from her shoe
The Devil taunts: with all his ploys
But she's true to me when we're with the boys
She may live in an ivory tower
But she always refreshes my wilted flower

# Cattle Drive Country

I am just an old country boy
From down town Texas way,
Just herding cattle that's how I earn my pay
Herd those critters they don't spook
Protect the chuck wagon and the cook
Dust clouds billow from the flailing hooves
A coloured kerchief hides my mouth but dust gets in my
eyes
My body is aching and tormented by the flies
The cook sounds the gong time for some chuck
Beans and beef jerky for evening tuck
Washed down by strong black coffee in a refill cup
When the drive is over, it's time to hit the town
A padre observes us with a disapproving frown
Expecting rowdy behaviour caused by the evil brew
Like drinking liquor from a loose woman's shoe
Letting off steam is what all cowboys do
Next year there will be a cattle drive repeat
Cos we mane lots of money selling cow carcase meat

# Owl

An Owl perched safely up a tree,
It's rotund eyes had much to see.
It let out an eerie screech,
On seeing prey for it to eat,
It soared high into the sky,
It plummeted down to make a kill,
Observed by onlookers standing stock still,
The victim in the throes of death,
Some sympathisers were left bereft.
It returned to its high vantage perch.
To disgorge pellets bone and fur.
This wily wise majestic regal bird,
If it's contented; too-wit too-woo to be heard.
This predator of the open skies,
With its acute rotund beady eyes

# Heartaches and Tribulations

Ballads tend to be about
A lost lover who broke their heart,
But where are the songs
About the loss of a best friend.
A type of heartbreak that TV shows
And the radio never prepare you for.
The heartache of losing your other half,
No one tells you about how much worse
A friendship breakup is more than a normal breakup.
Nothing can prepare you for that type of anguish
That you go through.
You go through the same stages as grief
Denial, bargaining, depression, anger, and then,
After a long time of healing, acceptance.
You feel as if your world has crumbled
Even though one day, they will be but a memory.
Whether they're remembered as good memories,
Or bad memories,
Is up to you!

# Order

How much love is there in you?
How much hatred?
In order for us to live
In a reality created by someone else's order,
Do you have to take from the people freedom?
I am not going anywhere,
Because in the name of your plans,
I will not orphan children!
There will be emptiness after me?
Everything has a beginning and an end.
Even war!
Dad, who are you talking to?
To myself,
Because no one wants to hear
What we are experiencing.
Sleep, my girl.
Should I be scared?
No! in this burrow underground,
death will not find us.

# The Price of Freedom

A ghostly image of a soldier
Stood in the background,
As a mother with a babe in her arms
Stood by a grave site.
She lowly whispered,
"Father this is your son.
Son this is your father.
He gave his life
So that others might live."
Now she is alone,
But she will survive.
She will raise this child
Without the aid of others.
This child will grow to be a strong man,
Because his mother was strong.

# To Lose You

You are my steadfast, you are my rock
You are my love ship, left in the dock
Your charm makes my heart just skip a beat
You can always be my surprise treat

*To hold you and feel your virile frame*
*To hold you so close will be my aim*
*Yet to lose you and be apart*
*That would break my heart*

A woman needs lots of warm affection
That's when we both achieve pure perfection
Marriage vows say to have and hold
A woman's wants are man to hold

*To hold you and feel your virile frame*
*To hold you so close will be my aim*
*Yet to lose you and be apart*
*That would break my heart*

The tenderness of your loving kiss
Is sweet and sheer bliss
You make my legs go jelly weak
When we are dancing close, and cheek to cheek.

120

# Dying Ember

Wanting you seems to be my fate
Like burning coals lay in a grate
Won't you set my longing heart aglow?
Please don't reject me, don't say "No"
Can't we both do what we think is right
Light the torch and both ignite

Please now leave me, something to remember
The afterglow of a dying ember
Take me back to your home address
Embrace me with your warm caress
Wrap your arms around me good and tight
And hold me close all through the night

When your eyes begin to smoulder
Lay your head upon my shoulder
Fill me with heartfelt desire
Making love beside an open fire

Wanting you seems to be my fate
My burning coals lay in a grate
Won't you set my longing heart aglow?
Please don't reject me, don't say "No"

# Don't Hold Back

I long for you with all of my might
Your kisses seem to be just right
Please say, I'm on the right track
Give your all and don't hold back
I've tried to draw your attention
Too many times, too often to mention
Won't you please save my plight
And give me comfort through the night
I long for you with all of my might
Your kisses seem to be just right
Please say I'm on the right track
Give your all and don't hold back
The warmth of your masculine touch
Is what I long for ever so much
Please don't be so contrite
Entwine our bodies through the night
I long for you with all of my might
Your kisses seem to be just right
Please say I'm on the right track
Give your all and don't hold back
A love filled marriage I crave
For you, storm and tempest I'd brave
Mission improbable it's true
If suspicion gets the best of you
I long for you with all of my might

Your kisses seem to be just right
Please say I'm on the right track
Give your all and don't hold back
Give your all and don't hold back

# Homeward Bound

*Unpack your bedroll it's time to hit the sack*
*Get in some shut eye just lay on your back*
*See the moon is rising it's so wan and pale*
*Listen to a lone coyote's plaintive wail.*
No desert sun—the nights grow cold
Joints are stiff and aching—began to feel old
Dog tired and weary can't open up your eyes
Dust covered debris stench and laden with flies
Doggies getting restless the herds on the move
Now being a cattle man, you'll have to prove
Half broke broncs cut out of spooked steer
Lasso and hog tie show no sign of fear

Uncontrolled critters gotta stop the stampede
Caused by jealous sheep men because of their greed
Stash all your doodads in an old gunny sack
'cos homeward bound is where I'm heading back

Unpack your bedroll it's time to hit the sack
Get in some shut eye just lay on your back
See the moon rising so wan and pale

Listen to a lone coyote's wail.
Stash all your doodads in an old gunny sack
cos homeward bound is where I'm heading back

# Sedentary Vocation

With his intended chosen vocation
Be it a sedentary occupation
Day after day he would sit and write
His copperplate calligraphy far into the night
Notations and essays he would pen with a quill
If not for a nib impinged in a stem, he would use
A fountain pen or an inky ball point
Putting archaic implements out of joint
Then the key loggia or the typewriter face
Inkjet now takes their place
Sits in his chair that feels a little damp
Now suffers arthritis and writer's cramp
Day by day goes by without a quibble
Trying to decipher his own eligible scribble
The school he attended as a mere lad
Pupils now use a futuristic, sensory pad
When only a child just learned to talk
Had to learn to cipher with brush, crayon or chalk
Now he has this artistic gift at his hand
A long way from writing with a stick in the sand
It's quite easy to erase a pencil mistake
Although his body's tired, his brain's wide awake

# The Spider

The gossamer net
The leggy poacher casts
Needs a client to
Break his fast
The waiting spider
Bides his time
For a tugging
At his line
Emerges in a haste
For his supper taste
Ensnared forlorn sticky coped
Given enough hangman's rope
No hope for buzzing beast
Now a hungry spider's feast

# The Future Is Left to Fate

Our love is like a swan upon a Lake
As it glides along so sedate
But still the future is left to fate
I fret for her when we're apart
Unbeknown the longing in my heart
Our love is like a swan upon a lake
Try to test if our love is stable
To be together when we are able
But still the future is left to fate
Just to hear her contented sighs
The look of longing in her eyes
Our love is like a swan upon a lake
Her beauty cannot ever escape me
Only time will say what will be
But still the future is left to fate
Death alone will rent us apart
Bringing grief to an aching heart
Our love is like a swan upon a lake
But still the future is left to fate

# Lasting Romance

From our first meeting, I was attracted to you
Your youthful beauty before me, just grew and grew
Your sylph like body with added charm
Sent my brain ringing like a fire alarm

*When I walked over and I asked for a dance,*
*Was it the beginning of a lasting romance*
*Your tender body moved like a dream*
*1 felt like the cat who had been at the cream*
Chancing my arm I asked for a date
You agreed and asked where to wait
There we would meet and go for a meal
Then I would try to amour you with my glib spiel

So close together so snug and warm
You made me happy a joy to be born
In the car, later I stole my first kiss
Your consent made my life bliss

There's nothing to compare with true romance
From our first meeting and our first dance
Brought together by the hand of fate
Togetherness was at last was worth all the wait

# Point Me in the Right Direction

When you kiss me, you're the most
If it weren't for you, I'd give up the ghost
I'll pop an invitation in the post
It's my party cos I'm the host

*Point me in the right direction*
*Its only for you I have affection*
*You are my number one selection*
*Baby you are sheer perfection*
If your lonely and on your own,
You know my number pick up the phone
I will call when you're at home
I don't want you to be alone

The nearness of your feminine charm
Makes me want to chance my arm
All you have to do is keep very calm
I won't let you come to any harm

When I'm with you, I feel content
Those happy times and memories spent
Just shout and I'll come hell bent
To be near you I'd pitch a tent

# Birth of a Baby Boy

Let's spare a thought for those now grown old
Shelter and warmth to keep out the cold
Choristers in unison their carols do sing
As one year ends what another may bring
Remember, remember the time of year
Of season's greetings and good cheer
Family gatherings that all enjoy
Commemorating the birth of a baby boy
To sit and dine on festive fare
A moment that one and all can share
Opening cards and gifts we like to receive
In Christian fortitude, let us believe
Remember, remember the time of year
Of season's greetings and good cheer
Family gatherings that all enjoy
Commemorating the birth of a baby boy
Let us pray to the Lord our sins to forgive
And to protect us whilst we do live
And when the day arrives and it's time to die
Our souls ascend to heavens high

Remember. remember the time of year
Of season's greetings and good cheer
Family gatherings that all enjoy
Commemorating the birth of a baby boy
The birth of a baby boy

# The Magi Came with Gifts of Praise

One starry night in Bethlehem a holy child was born
In a lowly cattle shed that early Christmas morn
The Magi came with gifts of praise
For this infant much acclaimed
They praised and blessed the swaddling babe
Jesus Christ, as he was named
This infant of such tender years
Became a carpenter by trade
He himself was nailed upon the cross
When his enemies did vilify degrade,
The Magi came with gifts of praise
For this infant much acclaimed
They praised and blessed the swaddling babe
Jesus Christ, as he was named
A crown of thorns adorned his head
A martyr for all mankind
He arose again, as from the dead
To leave the past behind
The Magi came with gifts of praise
For this infant much acclaimed
They praised and blessed this swaddling babe
Jesus Christ, as he was named
Make Christmas day a happy day if friendship does abound
Wish no ill on your fellow man

Let bigots flounder till they drown
The Magi came with gifts of praise
For the infant much acclaimed
To praise and bless the swaddling babe
Jesus Christ, as he was named
Remember the dead, but be proud of life
With kinship and festive cheer
Let's all pray to God to end such strife
And rid the world of fear
The Magi came with gifts of praise
For this infant such acclaimed
They praised and blessed the swaddling babe
Jesus Christ, as he was named.

# Please Love Me

I memorise your lies don't tease me
With hate and love from the very start,
I want you in my arms please, please me
I want you always, I don't want us to part
Please love me, please love me, darling how I cry for you
Tender memories, tender memories, how I long to be with
you
Just remembering your kissing
That is the thing we ought to do
That's what a kiss is, that's what bliss is
When I am holding on to you,
Please love me, please love me
Darling, how I cry for you
Tender memories, tender memories
How I long to be with you
Please love me, please love me,
Darling, how I cry for you
Tender memories, tender memories,
How I long to be with you
Please love me, please love me,

Darling, how I cry for you
Tender memories, tender memories,
How I long to be with you
How I long to be with you

# No Matter What You Say, You're Mine

We live our lives like hawk and dove
You don't seem to return my love
We used to go together like hand and glove
Now all you do is push and shove.
All I can do is bide my time
Guess you don't know where to draw the line
Keep me waiting I'll be just fine
No matter what you say you're mine.

I've had enough of your fornication
Telling me, I don't know my station
Discovering your lies was a revelation
You treat me like a poor relation.

Why on earth do you bring me untold shame?
I've had enough of your little game
You've had your moments of self-acclaim
Please won't you take me back if I'm to blame?

We live our lives like hawk and dove
You don't seem to return my love
We used to go together like hand and glove
Now all you do is push and shove.

Why on earth do you bring me untold shame?
I've had enough of your little game
You've had your moments of self-acclaim
Please won't you take me back if I'm to blame?

# My Lonely Mississippi Belle

My lonely Mississippi Belle
I wanna say I think you're swell
Do you like me? I just can't tell!
Please don't try and give me the hard sell
When you talk, my ears start burning
It's only for you I have that yearning
We're like two lovers who's only learning
Just keep those river boat paddles turning
I'm like a steamboat up the creek
And when you're near me, I just can't speak
Oh wanting you makes my knees go weak
Say we both hit a lucky streak
Losing you would hit me very hard
Like losing a gambler's ace trump card
So keep all your doors and windows barred
I hold you in very, very high regard.

Why can't we make our friendship gel?
My lonely little Mississippi Belle
Wanting you makes me so unwell
Won't you make a Riverboat Bell?
My lonely Mississippi Belle
I want to say I think you're swell
Do you like me? I just can't tell!
Please don't try and give me the hard sell

# Disciplined

Hope springs eternal, when I had to see the colonel
For a misdemeanour, I now regret
The commanding officer seated at his desk
In judgement of me for being a pest
This is not the first time you have missed reveille
Saying you were up late watching telly
Over sleeping is of no excuse
When in fact you had imbibed the devil's brew,
I deduced that you are a drunken sot
Any repeat of this offence, tolerate I will not
I award you seven days confined to barracks
Report to the guard room daily for midday roll-call
The provost will check your equipment and regimentals
You will be then doubled repeatedly round the barracks
square

# Drug Scene

Uppers, downers, benders, twisters
God's words proclaimed in scriptures
Inhale cannabis just get a whiff
And enjoy a soothing relaxing spliff

The law comes down hard upon the drug scene
Inject a dose of heroin or keep it clean
To still the nerves with illegal narcotic
And have illusions and thoughts of the psychotic

Partake in dope and amphetamine pills
Reputed to calm, and alleviate, all mental ills
Take a tube to sniff up powder or cocaine certain to befuddle
and inflame the brain.
Inject heroin into the arm by hypo needle
until the body becomes weak, frail and feeble

Marijuana is legal in California U.S. State
What transpires in Britain we can only sit and wait
Touts and pushers trade their insidious wares
For naive and vulnerable, let's say our prayers
Methadone a drug substitute to placate junkies when
addicted receive treatment by medical staff to be praised and
congratulated

Touts and pushers trade their insidious wares
For naive and vulnerable, let's say our prayers
Methadone a drug substitute to placate junkies when
addicted receive treatment by medical staff to be praised and
congratulated

139

# Burning Ambition

Be it my final decision
Is to achieve my heartfelt ambition
To record my demos be it country or pop
And to reach the chart's number one spot

Ditties and lyrics in the back of my mind I try to formulate
with a story or rhyme
A catchy melody or melodious treat
A toe tapping musical harmonious beat

Is my furtive vocal final ambition
The crowds all sway together and join in unison
Creating a chart topping raucous din
Ambition to create a saleable audible noise

This can be offered to the public
An ambition since we were just mere little boys
Now the band play together maestro's have gelled
They play over the airwaves achieved their long-standing
ambition.

# Chaste

The boy seemed to have taken a shine to me
Should I placate him and ask him to tea
If a girl takes up the challenge, is it effrontery showing your
conquest to the family

Is he a mere dance partner or a prince?
Finding romance with a glass shoe
A comforting arm around the waist
A tentative little squeeze, as she is so chaste.
Holding hands as we walk at a gentle pace,
Sheer naivety in the human race

When she succumbs to your masculine ardour.
Sometime soon he's to be a dotting father.
Don't try to take my strong handsome beau,
We are a matched couple I want you to know,
Go and look for other fish to fry,
Now I am the apple of my lovers eye